HOW
THE
LOSERS
LOVE
WHAT'S
LOST

HOW
THE
LOSERS
LOVE
WHAT'S
LOST

Patrick Ryan Frank

FOUR WAY BOOKS

TRIBECA

Please direct all inquiries to:
Editorial Office
Four Way Books
POB 535, Village Station
New York, NY 10014
www.fourwaybooks.com

Library of Congress Cataloging-in-Publication Data

Frank, Patrick Ryan.
  How the losers love what's lost / Patrick Ryan Frank.
     p. cm.
  ISBN 978-1-935536-20-8 (pbk. : alk. paper)
  I. Title.
  PS3606.R384H69 2012
  811'.6--dc22

                              2011027992

This book is manufactured in the United States of America
and printed on acid-free paper.

Four Way Books is a not-for-profit literary press. We are grateful for the assistance
we receive from individual donors, public arts agencies, and private foundations.

Funding for this book was provided in part by a generous donation
in memory of John J. Wilson.

This publication is made possible with public funds
from the National Endowment for the Arts

and from the New York State Council on the Arts, a state agency.

Distributed by University Press of New England
One Court Street, Lebanon, NH 03766

We are a proud member
of the Council of Literary Magazines and Presses.

CONTENTS

for my father, the hunter

A RUNNER STUMBLES

Heavy was the paper number pinned
upon my back. Heavy were the eyes
upon me. Heavy were my bones and black
the asphalt, hard and rising swift like water
in a flooding car, like anger in the back
of someone's throat. It seemed so clear: the motion
underneath it all, the lines laid out,
each step unto the next, into the near
expected. I understood. And then I fell.
And from the world I fell into the world.
I fell with the sound of a long rope breaking,
a sound that sounded much like distant yelling,
like drunks, like priests ill-cassocked in their faith,
a father, sleepless all these weeks, who takes
the crying baby, who gives her one quick shake.

THE PEOPLE IN THOSE PLACES

Getting undressed, the prostitute smiles
   at the boy, his knock-down wonder,
   naked and waiting under
the covers. Only a couple of miles
   away, the big jets thunder

into and out of O'Hare. But here,
   at the Beggar Moon Motel,
   in this room with its cigarette smell,
a man in a charcoal suit can hear,
   through the wall, the hooker tell

the boy how gentle she's going to be.
   Staring at nothing ahead,
   the businessman on his bed
listens, waiting quietly
   for what comes next. Instead,

he hears a cleaning lady sing
   as she scrubs a stain on the floor
   outside his bolted door.
He thinks the whore is singing something
   to the boy she's with; the more

he hears, the more he's sure the boy
   is lying against her breasts,
   eyes closed, her fingers pressed
to his cheek as she sings him to sleep. Annoyed
   with the stain but doing her best

to get through the shift, the maid in the hall,
   down on her hands and knees,
   sings in Portuguese
and thinks of her husband, imagines the small
   penny-thin sound of his keys

 as he takes off his clothes to get into bed.
   In his room, the businessman
   listens as close as he can.
He imagines himself with the hooker, head
   in the pillow of her hands

as she sings to him, only him.
   He falls asleep as the light
   of the hotel's blinking white
half-moon sign extends past the rim
   of the city, graying the night.

WORD FOUND TRACED ON A FROSTED WINDOW

Me—and nothing else, nothing less
than the tip of a life with all its flourishes:
perhaps a pair of patent-leather boots;
a year spent sending letters to married men;
perhaps a flaring smile, a stick-sharp grin
in the back of strangers' vacation photographs;
someone restless, perhaps, but not yet reckless;
a sly cartographer creating a town
that has never existed, near some minor border:
a speck, a word to pin the map in place.

FRANCISCO DE ORELLANA IN THE UNMAPPED JUNGLE

We drift and drift. What bit I sleep,
I dream of the city: the pyramids' steep
gold steps, gold pillars, terraces;
gold domes like the breasts of Doña Inez,
smooth, half-savage, chambers that keep

the caches every Christian man
covets but cannot understand.
But the shrubs and vines on the riversides
are as thick as brick and mortar. We've tried
to cut new trails, but I haven't a man

willing to leave the river, afraid
of the natives and their demons that wait
in the places God has not yet gone.
As the current drags us on,
I fear we might have floated straight

past the city already, missed
the flash of gold among a twist
of moss and orchids. We've turned
the boat around, tried to return
to Quito, but the current resists

us and we've lost too many to row
against it. Rust has begun to grow
on my armor and my arquebus.
Serpents and flies are always among us,
and perhaps the chaplain's right: we go

down into the devil's garden; each
bend of the river, every reach
carries our barge farther from
the golden kingdom, into the hum
of mosquitoes, sickness, the awful screech

of monkeys and unseen scouts. The days
and jungle last forever, always
the same: grim rain and heat, green vines,
green trees and prayer. No city. No signs.
And everything moves. Everything stays.

SKINNY KID

A thin magician, master of the vanish,
the pulling back into a baggy shirt
until invisible: an empty seat
in the back of the room, a blank in trig or Spanish,
a silence when a teacher says his name.
And when he's seen, he's just a shape in the hall,
an acned smudge shoved up against a wall
and then forgotten, then thin air again.

No one sees him planning his next trick,
talking to himself behind that truck
in the parking lot—half pack of cigarettes,
twist of smoke, a practiced flick of the wrist—
feeling the weight in his pocket, weight in his fist,
held breath exploding in his hollow chest.

A GAMBLER PRAYS

May the first card laid
before me be an ace,
placed face-up and pointing forward
toward a king. May I raise

on every hand, the men
around me folding. Let
the waitresses all be redheads, thin
and grinning, gathered to watch me bet.

May the roulette wheel
be whirling fast as the blade
of a helicopter letting down
its long white rope, that it may sway

into my open hand,
and lift me through the night,
leaving the dealers looking up
to see me rising out of sight.

And if, at dawn, I'm found
face-down in the fountain, may
I be laid on the game room's soft green lawn
of carpet, that my name be played

on the harps of the slot machines,
pooled in the players hearts,
and let my eyelids be left open
that I may see those flaring lights.

FIRST RUNNER-UP

I thought my heart would stop when he said my name
too soon. Suddenly, I'm the one moved over,
girl cut in half by the photograph's hard frame,
remembered, if at all, as a blank of silver

lamé and a small bouquet of lilies, off
to the side of the stage, practicing my smile
for all the almost-pretty girls on the rough
edges of the slow parade-route mile.

As the music gushes and the tiara's placed
elsewhere, I tell myself there's still a chance
that something big will happen, that I'll be raised
suddenly, as if in rapture. I can't

let myself be angry. I won't believe
this is the first step down to the rest of my life.

A MOTHER, THE BREATH GONE OUT OF HER

Does anyone know—
                    the moment gone beyond
your reach, the minutes on the back porch shouting
at the shivered wheat, gold waste without an echo.

Somewhere, a thick locked door and tread-worn stairs
go down and down and still—
                    oh god—
                                        go down
into the darkness, track of that black magnate
vanishing with those bones into the dirt,
pulling at the roots—
                    Already too late,
the police and their apologies, the pale
neighbors standing there, the absolute
weight of waiting for anything to happen.

Open every window to the cold:
the countless moaning mouths, a long low tone;
every single living thing sings *No—*

THE 6TH OF JULY

This is the night before the encierro.
Pamplona is crushed with tourists. The bars are full.
The iron gates are up across the narrow
side-street archways. The boys are dancing boleros
for San Fermín, dragged to God by a bull.
They'll sing all night. Nobody wants to die,
but bravery's like a sunburn: for anyone
to see it, it must hurt. They wait for the sun
to rise. Each bull dreams of a soft white thigh.

AWOL

Not another bus till one.
The soldiers in the station's john
  are going to pierce each other's ears
with bourbon and a service pin.
  Something in the row of mirrors

is wrong. They notice, but they can't tell
precisely what it is, what detail
  is missing, and they don't talk about it.
The private blackens his pin with a small
  white lighter and makes up jokes—*How did*

the Arab pay the whore?—but they
are wondering just how and why
  things changed: holes in their hometowns
have opened, the plastics factory
  and bars are somehow strange, the fairgrounds

and city parks all different, odd
in their heads, whole years relit with doubt.
  It isn't even close to one.
The station bums walk in and out.
  The one gone thing goes on being gone

among the stalls and tiles, the rough
graffiti. They watch each other laugh
 in the mirrors. The pin catches the light.
The corporal says, *We'll do the left.*
 If that looks wrong, we'll do the right.

SINGLES' NIGHT AT THE ART MUSEUM

A roomful of places to turn, every picture
a picture of conversations waiting to happen:

the paramedic with his trauma jargon,
a lawyer, a doorman, store clerks, one thin woman

with half a dozen stories about the things
she's accidentally swallowed. That nervous boy

in the enormous sweater would follow anyone home
who'd let him, walking just a step behind.

The men refuse to stand beside the nudes.
The women refuse to speak to each other and most

are silent, thinking of the things they'll say
about the saturation of the colors,

the way those lines don't intersect. Here
is a painting of an almost empty sea.

Here is a woman laughing, or maybe she's not.
Here is a tin pail overflowing with apples.

A WEIGHT IN THE BALANCE

The man on the steps, his head against the rail,
asks you for money, and you, a sudden liar,

say you haven't any. Walking on,
you wonder how many people mumbled no

and hurried past him, wondering who he was
before becoming that smudged-up thing they saw

on the street: a refugee from a personal war,
all grease and tatters, his face sun-burnt and raw.

Was he at home, sitting beside his pool,
watching the film of his life on its endless loop

when he realized that he could leave, the pets
barking wild behind him, every step

like water rushing through a broken dam?
He knew that he could let himself go mad,

carried along like debris in the river's flow,
or as hunger—raving, constant—pulls the wolf

through the winter emptiness, that angry tug
in the desperate, secret wasteland of the gut.

GHOSTS

Each of them missed his moment, felt it pass
like a body moving through an unlit room.
The grandfather clock clicks through the minutes, bangs
the hours, and they, in their old-fashioned hats

and dull black jackets, pace the upstairs halls,
practicing the words they should have said:
another *Stop*, another *I'll sober up.*
And in their murky heads, they run through all

the cues they missed, the marks they didn't hit.
Sometimes—on certain weeknights when it's rained—
they gather in attics, unused nurseries,
and they rehearse like actors. Together, they sit

and thumb their scripts, dog-eared and yellow. The play
is titled *Living*, and it starts in the dark
with a knock on a heavy door. Then, a voice:
Darling, darling, I have something to say.

THE GO-GO BOY DANCING ON STAGE

Some nights, my skin is so tight
it drums beneath that ragged beat.
I wear my boots and belt
filled with bills, number-scrawled
and small, so wet at the end
of the shift no taxi driver takes them.
Sometimes, I grin for a ten
or twenty, some young face in the light;
mostly, though, I dance
against the music and the hands
on my thighs, knowing they know
that later, when the music slows,
I'll lower myself to the crowd,
legs opening like a butterfly knife,
and hollow all of them out.

BROKEN BIT

Late afternoon in the low November light,
      a horse hard-ridden throws its rider.

Here, in the boundless nowhere of a meadow
      left fallow, the man and mare are thrown

into the moment between the dirt and sky,
      crack-jawed, red-tongued and fury-eyed.

The wind is in the switchgrass, clover flecked
      with spit and blood. The air is thick

with the man's wet cough and the horse's shudder, not far
      away, not running anymore,

stopped standing still by the sudden weight of the change
      that has settled on the thistle and grain.

The field is now a dangerous space, now strange,
      now each thing strains to gain a place.

MISSING-PERSON PHOTOGRAPH

He fell through the camera's well—black circle, deep—
through the polished outer half of the convex lens,
the color-corrective glass, the iris opened
to its widest aperture. The second half
of the lens refracted him; it pinned his arms
to the plastic film, his face in silver bromide
and gelatin, and there, in only one
one-hundred-twenty-fifth of a second, the boy
was kept in his white-striped shirt—still, intact,
exact forever—before the shutter dropped
and the photographer saw him sitting upright, smiling
in front of a dark-blue curtain, eager to leave,
leaving just that cobalt blank behind.

L'ARMÉE DES OISEAUX AFFAMÉS

Every Sunday morning, something's wrong—
strange weight that dwells inside the chest. At ten,

I walk down to the park and watch the swans
sail past the benches full of widowed men

in thick brown coats and caps. We get along,
the men and I; we sit all day, play cards

in silence, everyone collecting hearts.
When someone looks across the water, past

the white flotilla, as if to search the vast
lacework of clouds for something lost—a part

of the oddness of the day—I want to stand
and start the battle-hymn of lonely fellows,

to lead my little army of widowers
parading through the city avenues,

our banners rustling, heavy in our hands:
our symbol not the swan but a cormorant

in splendor, ready to devour each day,
black wings unfurled against an even gray.

Of course, that never happens; we just play cards.
The game goes on a while, and when it's over,

we go to our homes and sit beside our windows,
looking down at the streets—no wonder there,

no wonder coming around the corner.

GUN MOLL

I wasn't going anywhere in that town
until he came, his smile as smooth as tin
and just as sharp. My sister calls it sin
and shakes with envy. Each bank job feels like the sun
breaking through clouds; he says that what we've done
has lit me up, and I come grand as dawn
among the hostages, as if walking down
a chapel aisle in a yellow gown
to take his hand, heavy as a gun,
to show him where to go from where we've gone.

CALIGYNEPHOBIA

The fear of beautiful women.

Everybody knows the type:
      a man who, when he sees
a woman with long red hair, with hips
like foreign music, open lips
      like candy, turns and flees

while his buddies laugh and introduce
      themselves to the woman, who's new
to town and really very nice.
A fellow who, whenever he tries
      to talk to that girl with tattoos

on her hands and hard sharp Swedish cheeks,
      stammers on about
his nightmares bright with fires, speaks
in a little voice, high and weak,
      or else gets nothing out.

Each night, alone, he hits his head
      against the bedroom wall,
again, again, shaking the bed
as if in sex, breathless, face red,
      trying to hammer that nail

of his desire into the board
           of the beautiful world, on which
to hang his crumpled hat. But the wood is hard;
he hits with all that built-up hurt
           and still can't leave a scratch.

PROFESSOR MORIARTY ADDRESSES THE CLASS

And here is the final problem: a body falls
from a foreign cliff. The drop is ninety feet,
and if the wind is nothing and the lucid Alpine air
is dry and Celsius seventeen degrees,
how fast will he fall? How hard will he finally hit?
Let's say the man is roughly fifty, thin,
my height in brand-new boots and not athletic—
never set foot in a dance hall, never danced
a step, too slight to be a fighter, fingers
stained with ink, unlikely to keep a grip
on the granite edge. And if he spins his arms
the way a falling person always does—
strange whirligig, suddenly so heavy—
how much time will he have to ponder his years,
his victories, that little gaslight pride
that flares within his skull and does not go out
even as the air is rushing up
around him, catching his great black coat, not
enough to save him, no, but still enough
to slow his wild acceleration just
a little, maybe an inch per second per second—
Yes, it matters! These are the true mathematics:
the seven bleeding knuckles, the weight of the skull,
the mass and angle of the rocks below,
the words that break in his head as they approach.

JUST SOME NOISE

So a boy and girl are necking in their car,
parked in the dark of some back road. They hear
a sound like scratching, no, like someone breathing.
She had been nervous to begin with: this
was finally happening, but in the car
with a boy who wasn't all that pretty, even
in dashboard light. And he was anxious, too,
imagining the tender hooks of her bra
and how they'd hold, and how they'd come apart.
So when they hear—or think they hear—that noise,
they're half-relieved. They separate, sit straight,
and she demands they leave. He turns the key
and floors it back toward town, away from that sound,
away from that weightless moment, her mouth, his hand
beneath her shirt. But when he takes her home
and she gets out and screams at her car-door handle,
at the gleaming, torn-off hook, he doesn't think
before he pulls her panicked shoulders close
and holds her; and he becomes the handsomest man
she's ever known—so solid, safe and whole.
But back beside the road, a one-handed man
is crying. Nothing ever turns out right—
that careless second with the circular saw
while making a gift for a girl: a heart-shaped frame
he'd never finish, never fill. Bad luck

and circumstance: no money for prosthetics,
just a metal hook and medications
against the stares, unfriendly bar-stool questions,
the years of wanting to hold a woman's hips.
Now this: sore-armed in the dark, embarrassed, cold,
when all he wanted was that little thrill
of seeing people happy, just that one
little sliver of someone else's fun.

WEREWOLF

I am not always what I am.
I drive straight to work and home most days; most nights,
I laugh at the TV and I go to bed. But when the light
is strange and the screen door slams

in the wind, I can't sit still or sleep.
I need to leave, become a shape in the dark
of parking lots and parks,
the streets outside of bars. I keep

myself hidden and wait. My wife can't know.
I don't want her scared, to shudder when we're together
and the lights go out. I wouldn't hurt her
if I could help it, but I have to go

when hunger hits. My hands
begin to itch, begin to clench, and I can't think
about anything
except that crescent of skin between the shirt and pants

of someone lifting his arms, someone narrow-eyed,
breath ragged, blood drumming
in our chests as he sees me clearly, sees me coming:
hair and muscle, mouth that opens, opens wide.

AND SUDDENLY, THE ENDLESS EARTH

Busy, his mother didn't hear
　the screen door swinging shut.
Outside, the cricket chirp was clear;
　the grass had just been cut;

day-heat dulled in the sugared air.
　The boy continued past
the clothes-lined sheets, past the pair
　of lilac bushes, the last

tame things before the fields began—
　fallow acres of clover,
rag and milkweed tall as a man,
　pollen heavy over

everything. He parted the dense
　unthreshed field grass, which spread
past a bent-down barbed-wire fence
　and into the distance ahead.

No one, nothing, noticed him,
　only all that sky,
all that careless blue undimmed—
　an ever-emptying eye.

THE MAN LIKE AN EMPEROR MOTH

The summer pins him down, the sun one end
of the straight pin sticking him against the earth,
uncovered and vulnerable, convexed by the mirrors
of the boys' sunglasses like television sets
that might switch suddenly on. Everything
is watching him, closely, and everywhere,
following the colored wing of shame
that trails behind him, broken in some crime
forgotten just the moment it was committed.
If only he knew what he had done, he thinks,
he could enjoy the vanity of guilt,
dress himself in his own ruthlessness—
inscrutable coat, a cap to shade his eyes.
And then, at last, they'd feel him staring back.

HOMOPHOBIA

The fear of homosexuality.

It never made any sense—confusion of skins,
the muddled parts, the way one body sinks

into another, vanishes, how things
fit themselves together. His teenage nights

were dense with dreams: the chlorine stink of the pool,
wet skin of the boys playing water polo,

laughter heard under water. He woke up tired
every morning. During college, he tried

to do it right—meeting girls in bars,
the hurried drunken necking, fumbling with bras

in bathrooms, hoping his needs and wants would weld
together. He took to porn, the slick and lewd,

Hustler, catalog of genitals,
too scared to buy the hard stuff, sometimes stealing

videos with their calm parade of erections,
relentless, unapologetic secretion

of lust, the permutations of actors, each
combination of bodies making him ache

with an idiot throb, making him hate being
inside himself, not knowing how to begin,

when or where to look. Evenings in parks,
on benches near bushes, waiting for a spark

to catch and burn him up; the stares and sad
half-smiles; eventually the personal ads,

the lists of men wanting to get laid.
He told himself he only had to dial

and talk a bit. That's all. It didn't mean
that anything would happen, just a name

on an answering machine, just a waste
of time, most likely. His palms were smooth with sweat

as he dialed, slowly, leaving naked rifts
between the digits. Answered on the first

ring, the call was quick. Tim lived on a lane
of close-built stucco houses. He was short and lean

and gentle—Tim led him to a bed with a blue
bedspread, showed him how to use the lube,

how to hold his legs. His body burned,
and it was almost like the loss of a burden.

They finished and he left. They never met
again, but soon there were others: an EMT

with wide-set eyes, a couple of married salesmen,
a lawyer on ecstasy and several nameless

balding men he met at a highway rest stop,
sitting for hours in his parking spot.

Even the quickest ones were nice—attentive
and careful, every movement tentative;

but, each time, he felt like a meteor
burning against resistance: falling, remote.

His mind would wander to bills, the videos rented
and waiting to be taken back. Each tender

touch, each kiss pushed him farther outside
of his skin. Their sweetness came to be tedious,

and he didn't know why. He tried rough trade: a marine,
volunteer firemen, a couple of drunken airmen

he took to an alley—guys who didn't care
if he got off, who only wanted to race

to the finish and get away from him, no trace
of feeling. He hoped to force his heart to react:

to either welcome humiliation, defer
to a stranger's pleasure, be used; or else be freed

and finally able to want something deeper.
But still it didn't happen. Each time he peered

into the depth of his body, where desire
and all its painful turnings used to reside,

all he saw were disappointments, lost
anticipation, the junk of parking lots

and hectic chat rooms. He gave up. He had tried
to find rapture and failed, and now he was tired

of all of it. No more men or the lows
of sex and after, wanting to want, the slow

disaster of coldness. It wasn't easy to bear
being alone, but simpler than the bare

hours with strangers and their earnest strain.
Quiet months, and then, when changing trains,

he saw a guy who looked familiar: thin
and all sharp angles, hazel eyes, a hint

of some small sickness. He wasn't wearing a ring,
and when he caught him looking, there was a grin

as white and broad as panic. He felt a surge
of something warm, an echo of those old urges

he'd struggled under. When they reached his stop,
they both got off. Pages of the *Post*

rustled like birds through the station in the quiet
after the train, when they were not quite

alone. The man came up and touched his elbow
and said, *Hello*. There was a twisting below

his heart; he felt himself make a fist,
saw it hit the man where the jawbone fits

into the skull, felt that sudden leaden
weight against his knuckles. The moment leaned

forward in silence. He saw the man's hands swing
upward, closing, as the paper wings

lifted away around them; saw the man's arm
crashing into his chest; felt it ram

into him over and over. He collapsed,
cradling his head, onto the scalloped

concrete, waiting for the rest. The man left
after a moment and people came over. He felt

that it should have hurt more than it did. Now,
hours later, walking on his own

through some dark neighborhood, he wonders how
it ever works. There must be someone who

could tell him, if he knew how to ask. He'd listen
to every word. But the night just gets more silent,

and no one's around—just dark parked cars, street lamps,
concrete cracked like lines in an old man's palms.

IT ISN'T PARANOIA IF IT'S TRUE

An empty wheelchair in an empty park,
parked car packed full of children's toys—I can't
quite shake the feeling things are happening
to other people, either miracles
or somethings awful, but not to me, as if
my name is off the list for some event
the universe is having: massive party,
prison riot, something half the town
has found an invitation to, like money
in a brand new jacket pocket, like bits of glass
in a cereal box, but I still have some hope
I'll open a door and find a room of people,
all strangers, shouting, *Surprise,* shouting, *Look out!*

A ROOMFUL OF WIDOWS

No one understands how hard it is
to find a veil these days. Ask the widows

where they got theirs and they'll just shake their heads.
You have to find out for yourself. Ask

the widows anything and they'll just smile
or tell a story: how they used to drink

too many daiquiris on weekends, how
they used to think that black was thinning, but now—

The room is full of interruptions. They hold
each other's hands, admire each other's pearls.

They touch each other's taffeta and lace.
And when they move, they make a noise like a broom

being pulled across a beach-house floor.
And when they laugh—more often than you'd think—

it sounds like wind chimes falling to the ground.
And they keep hanging them back up again.

CARTHAGE, ILLINOIS

The postcards here have pictures of the jails:
    Old Mormon Jail, the Courthouse Jail;
or the murdered Brothers Smith; some with the war
    memorial engraved with *For*
            Our Sons, Our Sacrifice;
    a sketch of William Fraim, bright noose
            pulling at his neck.
People can be proud of anything.
    Even punishment. Leaving
            the spinning postcard rack
by Wear Drug's door, a man could walk a block
    down Walnut, left on Madison, walk
Buchanan to where the shuttered storefronts turn
    toward the sudden soybeans, new corn.
Green, intensely, and a scent like salt.
            So vast, and all so flat.
            A man could feel so tall,
he might let himself become convinced
    that he could do whatever he wants
            and get away with it all.

WE LIVE TO LOVE YOU MORE EACH DAY

Jayne Mansfield's epitaph.

Each day was a walk on the beach
in three-inch heels. The hair,

the lips, the hips and breasts,
the blush—it wasn't easy

looking easy, reaching
for those dangled grapes in a dress

with a broken clasp, giving
people what they wanted,

making them want it more.
Her shoulders ached, her back

was sore, but still the preacher
in the chapel of her chest

rambled on on sin,
on her place in a world that spun

on money and skin, on girls
like her: Miss Photoflash

and Miss Magnesium Lamp;
a blonde lit up with fame,

another Marilyn,
another Mamie, but maybe

more. Jaw locked and bending
forward for the cameras

so that they'd see her face
halfway between the cleavage

and the edge of the frame—Jayne
who painted; Jayne who played

piano, violin;
Jayne, young mother of five

and good at puzzles, bad
with husbands; lovely Jayne

who spoke five languages
but no one heard a word,

just that practiced laugh,
just the lift of her chest

which meant, *And here we are.*
And where was that? The dark

of Mississippi, outside
a stranger's house. A voice

that said, *Look at those stars.*
Then silence. Then, *Here's the car.*

AND SUDDENLY, THE ENDLESS EARTH

There wasn't anything on TV
  and all his books were read.
Outside the window, he could see
  his mother's garden, the shed,

the barns and then the corn and hay.
  He saw a dim sky riddled
with sparrows. Everything spread away
  from where he sat: the middle

of the bad last month of summer vacation
  with just the news and shows
he'd seen before, and between the stations,
  the endless falling snow.

INMATE

The sudden trials, verdict, the future cut
to the size of a concrete cell, and then the prison,
as real and awful as a gunshot gut—
I thought I'd die. But then I learned to listen

to the others joking, whistling, all their low
rough whispers at night. I rarely speak; I've burned
clean through that hectic oil. I've come to know
the subtle humor of the cells and learned

the lock-tight punchlines of the prison staff
walking their rounds. I've taught myself to wait.
To bear the wait, I've taught myself to laugh,
to laugh with a joy so hard it sounds like hate.

GIVEN A GIFT CERTIFICATE TO A FORTUNE TELLER

She said I had the saddest hands in town,
my palms like movies made from Russian plays:

bad lines, bad lines. She offered me a discount
on crystals and a candle to light my way

into my unlit future. The cards were laid
face-down across the table, and when I picked,

she started to laugh. A private joke, she said,
and then got serious—poverty and sickness,

misunderstandings. She offered me some water.
She said I'd want it later. She said I'd travel,

far but only briefly, like her daughter
who joined the navy and came home with a lover

with an ugly aura: awful mauve, some yellow.
Mine was muddy, but when she dimmed the lights,

it got much better. We built two piles of pillows
on her living-room floor and spread my astral charts

between us: here, the star of my birth; here,
my death. They looked the same. Here were the stars

above us then—that strange cold moment—clear
and terribly small in all that space, so far

from everything else. She pointed out my planets
in their shadowed houses, then she showed me hers:

Neptune, potential; Saturn, disappointment;
her daughter and the men, her Pluto, Mars.

She talked about her visions; her voice got deeper:
a leaking bowl; a high plateau, so bare

and very dry. She said she couldn't sleep
most nights because of what she knew, or feared

she might find out. She said to stay another
hour or so, no charge, and then we both

were quiet quite a while, watching the moths
against the window—so pale, so almost nothing.

VIRGINITY

Now just a half-remembered teenage strain:
strange pains, so much emotion; bedrooms, basements
where he exercised his heart to build it, make it
beautiful, as big and full as the life

he was sure he'd shortly have, his body bursting
into it like the varsity boys ripping
through the paper hoop and into the gym,
everybody shouting for the great

unstoppable. He can't recall exactly
moments, the months and one long edgeless grudge.
He knows that there were parks and parties, trips
to other towns. He knows there was a time

when just the thought of the sex he'd someday have
was enough to knock the breath right out of him.

HART CRANE IN THE MIDDLE OF THE SEA

Died after leaping from the deck of a steamship
that was returning to New York from Mexico, April 27, 1932.

His body pitched, hyperbola of noon,
arcing declination over the gunnel
and into that tangled sea, a skein of trouble
he'd always known so well. And as he fell,

he imagined, again, himself a native man,
a regnant boy, an unvoiced naked slave
running through the body-bruising waves
to greet conquistadors agog with lust

for this new land, this never-home he left
unwon. But his was the world of expatriates:
terrible siroccos, insistent breakers,
fell cities with nothing underneath the bridges—

only water, only ever water
and the body's obdurate throb of recollection:
the voyaging hull foam-licked, the purser's lips—
what strange unrest, redundancies of flesh. . .

He had met the bottom of the world,
and it was cruel, possessive, calling him
to that obscurest ocean, where everything
is welcomed, wanted, nothing is explained.

THE VET AT THE BUS STOP HAS SOMETHING TO SAY

That I was happy in the war.
Just that one great thing, and men
who understood it. Not like after.
I owned each inch of my body then,

rented to the Army; they paid
with the miles they put between my parents
and the rest of my life. They gave us crates
of oranges. They gave us tents

where we could eat them, where we could sleep
like mortars, deep and ready to blow
at the slightest need, or else not sleep
at all. All sudden. Not like now.

There were months of sun and birds in the air,
wet dreams and jokes that hit your gut.
Sure, people were dying there,
and that was enough to let you forget

the whole *back home*. Because this mattered.
Each of us no one, then the war,
and we were in front of the world. We mattered.
Each, just then, a movie star.

THE HUNTER

Lost in the mountain range
of the vitals screen: brain

and pulse, the hollow peaks
in green the green of pines,

in black like a rifle's bluing.
Each breath is small and slow

in his throat, as in the dark
of a morning when he pressed

his thick unwilling foot
into the boot, shrugged on

the orange vest and rushed
against the sun, knowing

that dawn, like sickness, starts
slowly, but then comes quicker.

Quickly, it's here; it lights
each tree, it lights each leaf,

the trail run down from the hills
and into a flat, wide field.

AND SUDDENLY, THE ENDLESS EARTH

Later, his mother called his name.
  His father searched all night.
In the morning, the neighbors looked, the same
  dull panic along the tight

brush-combing line. The hours smothered
  the town; everyone searched
for anything to bring to his mother
  pacing the length of the church.

She barely slept that first long week,
  hoping for any news
from the fields, the crew searching the creek.
  The wood grain of the pews

became a map, an elevation—
  a dark topography
of a vast, unknowable location
  where nobody could be.

VIRGINITIPHOBIA

The fear of rape.

They took her out to the field in a new black truck
       that smelled like apples and the denim

of a young man's thigh. They turned the engine off
       but left the radio on, the headlights

on woods to the west, toward the mountains, then
       to California. They laid her down

and tied her hands over her head with field-grass.
       She could have pulled them free, no problem,

ripped the roots right out of the soft dark dirt.
       They told her she was beautiful.

They took off their shirts. She saw the black of their arms
       backlit in gold by the truck's headlights.

One of them started to crack a joke, but stopped
       halfway in. They took off her shoes

and touched her ankles, only barely. She waited
       for them to lift the hem of her skirt

but they were scared and it was cold out there.
            She arched her back and held her breath,

eyes closed, but they kept saying they were sorry.
            She told them to shut the fuck up, and if

they started to cry, she'd kill them and take the truck
            and no one in town would ever know.

While they were kicking off their jeans, so slowly,
            she listened to the radio

and cicadas whirring like the circular saws
            in the high-school shop, and a distant hum

that could almost have been a train if trains
            still ran anywhere nearby.

It must have been an airplane flying low
            somewhere above. She couldn't tell

because it was cloudy and dark, which bothered her;
            she'd wanted them to see her face

moonlit and unforgettable, staring up.

CHARACTER ACTOR

Little better than an extra, I play
an unlovely face for laughs, go out of my way
to look for trouble: maybe I get sick,
or if I'm lucky, shot by some slick heavy,
and the heroine thrusts her chest, fists clenched, and cries.
And if the part is really good, I die
under the lights and orchestration. The movie
gives me that slow sweet close-up, before it goes
to whatever comes after that wet grass, those cellos.

WHAT I WANT FROM THE WORLD

On some bright beach in Hawaii,
in some dim year of the past,
one leper in love with another
says, *Take my hand*. That's all—
sweet joke or two, quick touch,
an elegy on a postcard.
Not much, no more than moments
of luck in a luckless life,
of trouble beautifully lit.
So let the lepers think
the numbness of their lips
is love. Let the sharks
be far and slow. Let
nobody see their bodies
as they run into the sea
with the sun in tatters on
the water, with laughter, a wind
through palms that sounds like *Please*.

THE THIRD-PLACE CONTESTANT ANSWERS
THE QUESTIONS THAT WERE NOT ASKED

Argentina. Aphids. Virginia Woolf.
A group of vultures circling the air
is called a kettle; on the ground, a venue.
Who discovered Pluto? Clyde Tombaugh.
Who was Sherlock Holmes's nemesis?
Professor Moriarty, a man who thought
he knew the answers, until he met a man
who did. Detroit. Potatoes. The Punic Wars.
The current tallest building in the country
is the Sears Tower. I went once to the top
and felt it swaying in the wind like rope.
What river flows over the rocks of Victoria Falls?
The blue Zambezi. How many feet in a meter?
3.281. What is the main
ingredient of gunpowder? Saltpeter.
It's white. It smells like books in a cardboard box,
or photo albums: all those pictures of kids
on beaches, wheat-haired girls. Someone's cousin.
Someone's uncle. No one recalls their names.

EMILIE BURIED

Emilie Neumann Muse
January 14, 1908 – January 23, 2006

As heat and darkness and the smell of dirt
closed tight around her box-bound body, what thoughts
settled themselves in her? English, German,
bass drum, hard-heeled shoes, the Reading trains,
the traffic—black hearts beating through the earth
to mask from her her absence from the world
that might, at any moment, forget she lived
and leave her there in that nothing grip, near panic,
with just a slender pipe run up for air,
singing softly, wordless with the blare
of a distant trumpet, singing her to sleep
in the pressing dark, singing her awake,
ninety-seven hours before she heard
the sound of shovels, sounds like whispered words,
all meaning resurrection. As they lifted
her windowed coffin, dancers, band, spectators
applauded. There she was—girl Emilie,
hunger-weak, light-blinded, still alive
and strong enough to step out from her grave
and wave to them, just twenty-eight years old,
gone impossibly far and then come back.
She told them all it hadn't been as bad
as they'd imagined, and no one believed her.
She let herself be buried several times,
for smaller crowds and shorter stretches, until,

after a few more years of stunts and shows,
she married a man named Muse and loved him, left
the daredevil life to raise her children, who
never heard a word about the risks
she took, the deaths she could have died. Only
when the kids were grown and safely past adventure
did she pull out the clippings of herself
flying with Alligator Jim, swimming
around Manhattan, being buried alive.
American Persephone, the girl
who went into the ground, alone and lovely,
to rise again, alone and beautiful,
over and over. Even through those years
of having kids and housework, she kept a bit
of that blackness in her body, boxed inside
her aging heart, both memory and promise.
And when, at ninety-eight, after all
those quiet decades, she faced again that depth,
going slowly down, she saw a girl
rising up to meet her, slim and pretty
in a cotton dress, singing beneath her breath.

A FATHER, HIS VOICE YELLED HOARSE

Anything—
          So long already, the sun
now almost down, there's still so much not done—
the field, the creek, far copse of trees, crow-dark
and crowded with beer cans, thorns, dead things
and dirty magazines, all faded, fat
with rain—
          what's that—
                    No one can do enough.
Not them. Not you. The dogs are in the corn,
barking through the rows, and there are men
in the ravine, and someone's in the barn,
but still there's more to do. Acres. Acres.

You know that there must somewhere be a mark
in the clay, some bit of ripped red cloth; but here—
where are you—
          nowhere—
                    what have you got—
                              nothing.

LAS MANOS DE JUAN PERÓN

Both hands were cut from the corpse of the
former President of Argentina, July 23, 1987.

Cold and holding each other in their sack
in the back of a pickup truck, burlap rubbing

against the knuckles, knuckles rubbed to bone,
closed in a cardboard box and locked in a safe

behind a student's desk, taken out
over and over, shown to someone's sister

with shrieks and laughter, endlessly shaken, moved
from house to house and hidden, wrapped in linen,

unwrapped at kitchen tables, stared at by children,
blackened fingertips upon one palm,

a chainsawed wrist against the other, whispers
in the rooms, rewrapped when the arguments started, shut

in their box against the shouting, separated
when the ransom went unpaid, the right hand carried

to Buenos Aires, buried with prayers in a garden
of beans and beautiful onions, the left left in

its cardboard box, hid beneath a bed
for years with a rosary and ammo clip,

until the house's occupants' arrests,
and then just gone, just disappeared, the box

as empty as a stadium after the match
is lost, as a plaza when the rally's over,

widows and workers dispersed, the soldiers dismissed,
the clapping done, the echo faded, gone,

not even someone to pull the posters down,
no one left to pick the pamphlets up.

PLUTO, UNPLANET

Dark, oh yes, and cold, but I had pull:
grand and godlike distance, unseen, unknown.
And now? Another speck in a far space full
of rocks and unimportant bodies? No.
If not a planet, I'll be something else:
I'll be the grackle on your window ledge.
I'll be the book that falls behind the shelf.
The white-haired stranger standing at the edge
of your wedding reception, whispering to myself.

TOWARD NEBRASKA AND AFTER

You'll have a long, flat drive in a borrowed car,
but there will always be the radio

to sing you through the landscape, and there will be
the landscape opened out around you: greens

and browns and billboards, off-ramps, truck stops, towns
and farmland, the irrigation and machines

and silos stuck like some hitchhiker's thumb
to the blue midwestern air. There will be hours

stitched up with highway dashes. There will be dust
and ditches. If you pick that hitcher up,

he'll let you talk for miles. You'll tell him who
you are and where you're going, why, why now,

how you once thought that people sometimes fixed
their broke-down pasts, if they knew when and how.

The car will hum its way past exit signs.
He'll tell you, *Listen, mister, that was now.*

That late in the day and at that speed, the fields
will seem all full of dogs, dull black and fast.

ACKNOWLEDGMENTS

I must thank my many teachers for their assistance with these poems
and their invaluable encouragement, especially: Michael Adams,
Thomas Cable, David Ferry, A. Van Jordan, Brigit Pegeen Kelly, Mary Kinzie,
Robert Pinsky, Rosanna Warren, and Dean Young. The Fine Arts Work Center
in Provincetown, Mass., the Massachusetts Cultural Council, and the
James A. Michener Center for Writers lent their support to this project,
and I deeply appreciate it. Thanks also to Alan Shapiro, for his keen eye
and kind words; my fantastic editor, Martha Rhodes, and everyone at
Four Way Books; my family, for their bemused appreciation; James Reed,
for years of encouragement; and my writing friends, too numerous to
name and too wonderful to ignore, for camaraderie and inspiration and
everything else.

Finally, I have to thank the editors of the following journals, where many
of these poems, in some version or other, originally appeared:
*Best New Poets 2008, Borderlands, Boxcar Poetry Review, Cincinnati Review,
Hampden-Sydney Poetry Review, Hayden's Ferry Review, Memorious, Poetry,
Redivider, River Styx, Roanoke Review, Slant, Smartish Pace, Subtropics,
Sycamore Review, Third Coast,* and *Willow Review.*

Patrick Ryan Frank was born and raised in rural Michigan. He received a bachelor's degree in theater and creative writing from Northwestern University, and master's degrees in poetry from Boston University and the James A. Michener Center for Writers at the University of Texas, Austin. He was twice a fellow at the Fine Arts Work Center in Provincetown, Mass. He currently lives in Austin.